CAFÉ DISSERTATION

CAFÉ DISSERTATION

by

D. James Smith

HPP
Hip Pocket Press

HIP POCKET PRESS
Orinda, California
2023

ALSO BY D. JAMES SMITH

POETRY:

Prayers for the Dead Ventriloquist
with an introduction by Dorianne Laux
(Ahsahta Press, Boise State University)

Sounds the Living Make
(S.F. Austin State University)

PROSE:

My Brother's Passion (Permanent Press)

PROSE, YOUNG ADULT:

Fast Company (Dorling Kindersley)

The Boys of San Joaquin (Atheneum)

*Probably the World's Best Story about a Dog
and the Girl Who Loved Me* (Atheneum)

*It Was September When We Ran Away
the First Time* (Atheneum)

Published by Hip Pocket Press
5 Del Mar Court
Orinda, CA 94563
www.hippocketpress.org

This edition was produced for on-demand distribution by
lightningsource.com for Hip Pocket Press.

Cover image: *"H" Street Grain Silos,* © Mikko Kangas
Cover design: Tyler Varian
Book design: Wayne Smith
Typeset in 11 point Minion

Printed in the United States of America.

ISBN: 978-0-917658-49-5

CONTENTS

For Bruce

WINTER

Come evening the sea
strides forward, the moon,
a goiter grown fat in the neck of a pine.

The dirt lane fails near cliffs where a crone
pets a shook terrier with whispers.
She rattles her cart of rumpled clothes,

one hand, gloved with rags,
a blackbird that flutters
toward you from the sleeve of her coat;

its two-fingered beak takes your last coin.
You've come here to think less of yourself,

to sense deer, mist, winter's living
specifics, and you linger, moving
slowly with a tide that thickens
as it wrestles up the estuary,

past a pasture of cars, rusting,
rotting into the ground
like teeth sunk in a row,

the strange cry of geese, surprising
as a flock of bicycle horns close
but invisible overhead, insistent, there,
then swallowed by time.

You turn back toward the motels
strung, glowing, along the curved edge
of highway and think of
the woman lying there,

moving in sleep, and fear
whatever it is riffling long
fingers through the trees.

RAIN & I

Still vast, lung-wet, I lie there awhile,
trickling out of the tiny cracks in my wrists.

I waken slowly, cold as the sea and remember.
Days I drove home weeping for nothing

I could name but the bruised afternoons coming down
or your wet hair in the evenings, pearls of perspiration

beading your ears, the nape of your neck.
Dark hallway and a bed at the back

and a night wind blowing rain sideways
sounding like tacks flung against the windows.

And we, there, rising and falling
with those birds in the wallpaper trees.

LETTER

Come, I say, wanting to get it right this spring
because where you are is always a vision
of April and you turning back from the sun-
white windows of that cafe, your mouth, still
in my mind, a chapel statue's smile. I understand
the quiet violence in your womb that I insisted,
killed us. Tonight, toeing the chest of a dead wren,
soft palace of ants that gnaw and dream of flying,

I know I should have told you
how I can slip off like daylight,
or how much I wanted to rise in a landscape
of my choosing—no surf of freeways, just
sky scratched by distant birds.
Out here a plague of tree rats traces the power lines;
like fears at dusk, they grow bold.
My neighbor told me to get a .22 or I'd never last.

He doesn't know the dead are still forever
sacred in the stations of the imagination.
By the time you'd get here the cold will have quit.
There's a room, a dresser and the invisible wires
of satellites to make you feel safe.
This isn't me breaking down again. Just kneeling
awhile in the fields of brown grass around here.
I found a half-sunk, plaster St. Francis

with bird-shit epaulets, counselor to sparrows and men.
Why not believe we have some grace coming?
Today's paper said the Madonna is appearing
in the gravel parking lot of a Rite Aid

near the border. Children tell she has a patience
that speaks of us eventually finding ourselves
in another life. Hasn't it always been this way?
What we require. Resurrection.

Tonight, stars are floating like sparks above the fire I set.
If she's really there, it's like a trace
of the kind smoke makes signaling transformation.
Listen, this is an old and open place. In the evening there's
something in the wind snapping softly like hung laundry.
And the sky? It could be a woman in glittering black,
one hand reaching down, touching the hole in my side,
one hand tipping the cradle of the moon.

NEIGHBOR

Coming over the hill, his ploughed field
smokes in the headlamps of the truck.
A dog's hoarse bark jumps between house and shed.

Standing on the wooden porch, fog bearding my face,
I realize if my neighbor's still here he won't answer.
Last time he was suddenly at the edge of the orchard
then gone back into the shape a tree's shadow makes.

The yard is lost to memory, the roses tied
dead along the leaning fence.
In the soft cold, a tiny wind rattles
the only stars—the necklace of light bulbs

strung, still burning above the back door.
Near an iron barrel of rain, rusting
against the stoop, some wild thing has lingered.

THE INSOMNIAC

Your eyes unstick to morning sparking
in the sycamores, scattering the swallows that clot there
      at dusk.
Tell me I can do this, today if I need to. Tell me. Half-dreamed,
      as just before sleep,
that tin-canned echo falls through your head, sudden
as a match tossed in the dark—and sometimes a kind of vision before you
      like a pattern
of gnats in the brilliance of sun-shafts on water. A pot of thick coffee
      and you can see
that student in the back, the red-headed one with the skin of flecked
      muslin and the soft-mouthed drawl
of slow-motioned questions he hopes to polish and keep. You can almost
      recall a life as simple. Years ago,
you watched from the office window a fine rain blowing, the first leaves
of the season waking to wind, and she called, long-distance,
      to say the tests had come back: her, *Come soon,*
smoked and brittle on the line. Remember after. That singular calm. Stars
      creeping out onto puddles to sleep. And you
at an upstairs window, looking down, taking your first instructions
      from the dead.

ABSENCE

She said sometimes she felt
like a house tacked to a cliff,
all her windows
open to rain,
the scent of sea
rising up from the cellar,
the foundation, sodden,
shifting.

She said my subject was nothing but loss.
I said, No, it is love,
not loving deeply enough the ordinary
until it's gone.

Even as a child I was held
by the swollen-throated silences
between cuts of Donizetti on an old LP,
wanted to live
in those slow revolutions,
my whole body nodding
with the beat of my heart.

I never noticed
the many voices of birds
coming from outside the bedroom window,
soft-scissoring open my sleep,
until the week I was pinned
with only the hospital's dead
terrarium air.

Listen: the wind threshing
the palms, upended and waving
like feather dusters, shaking off
a couple of orange and white pigeons,
their soft clatter,
fading.

When the wind dies, I stop,
unsure if I've just heard my name.
I breathe deeply, recalling the scent
of wet soil on her wrists and her hands.
I recall the little clay figures
my hands made as a boy
after my oldest brother's body came home
in a low-bellied plane, bruised cloud
out of the East I watched drifting
down from the Sierra.

When she left,
I should have given them to her,
each for a windowsill,
guarding the night:
Boy Who Says, Why Would You Go Where I Can't Follow?
Boy Who Says, Go Away, Rain,
Boy with a Hole for a Mouth.

WEST VALLEY DOG

In a place on the far western side of the valley, we were standing
       but ten paces from the truck,
plants and rocks there like thorned planets, crashed and half-sunken
       in clay, dry rattle of cicadas coming,
at once, as from a distance and near. It was somebody's black lab,
       back-end broken as we thought, not dead,
still heaving the same air that burned our throats, hot as brandy.
       You knelt to lay your hand
on its side, and I, strangely, recalled pressing my forehead
       against the warm, misted flank of a horse
that had carried me through a pass in the Sierra as a boy
       when there were things that I wanted to see.
A rug of flies bristled over the wet wound on its rump and the dog
       whimpered and tried to thrash
its head as if for leverage, as if to rise, but it was past that.
       You looked at me, strings of hair
beating about your face, blue of your eyes washed clean and forgiving
       so that I knew it was good
to be loved, though I caught myself wondering if this meant we'd forgo
       the bottle of wine and the time
we'd saved for ourselves, your room with the candle and the shadows
       flickering. I knew you went away
to sit in the cab, windows rolled up, because later you wouldn't
       have wanted this image of me persisting. I believe
you were thinking of the child I didn't want. I don't know what you think
       now. I was there just a short while,
not alone, but with the animal, with it wheezing and that shovel crossed
       over my shoulder like a gun, and a diamondback
I watched coiling quickly down a hole like an ugly regret,
       just a few sandstone clouds
shelved above the coastal range, offsetting threads of doves twinkling back
       the last of that light, all
in my head, then and now. And then swinging hard, I brought
       the darkness down.

I WAS ONLY

Coming from a deep sleep,
the drumming of rain on the roof
percolating down through the whole of me,
sogged and thrashing once and again,
not knowing it was the rain's grave singing,

the water, my own water
pressing the heart that has been
drowning for a long time, the tissue
sort of rubbery the doctor says.
I was quietly slipping into myself,

trying on my hands like a stranger's gloves,
the eyes not windows yet, feeling
my hair matted with leaves,
and the small nameless bird
under the eaves was crying out,

wanting to be found by another
of its species, I suppose. I was
working some kind of abstract slant
in my head, making the form
of my body the way a chair

may be imagined with care
for the shape of they that
may take it eventually; though
somehow I was much more
nearly like a man

stepping into the street
raising a tentative hand
to wave to someone, the world
slicing past, the blind traffic,
just then, mistaken for a friend.

RAIN IN THE FENCE

This morning the rain is in the fence,
bled deep into the grain
by one whole night's deluge.
Last night it was a silver wall I watched
a stray dog leap through.
I drifted out under the trees' dark pleasure.
Was it the street lamps' buzz and flutter,
or the rising grass-wet scent
released by earth and water
that brought back the old
neighborhood, the heart of town,
thick sycamore and oak,
down-hung, rotted with mistletoe?
So many years ago it shouldn't matter,
standing outside a bay window, rain
off the roof spattering my face, soaking
my hair and jeans, I watched
my parents in the front room
of their house, reading.
How small they seemed and like
strangers there, quiet in their box of light.
My mother, drawn by a shadow, perhaps,
moving in the window, looked up
to see me, a thin ribbon of water
running down the pane. She turned
to my father, slowly, so as not to
disturb him, to study him, smoking
in his chair, my eyes going with hers
to see how he'd always be, bent
to one of the books that held him.
And then, she looked away.

THE CALF

Child of a dying wind it lay
in the muck and hot, blond grass
below the dam and its strangled creek
that my boyhood friend and I
crossed that morning, determined
to flee the nuns' black habits and ink,
to claim all property, posted or not.

And I remember thinking the eyes,
pulled by crows and gone, might have
envisioned a wilderness complete.
I knew dogs could dream; why not cattle?

The flies under its tail, too furious
to be waved away, seemed to be trying
to tunnel up under the tail where coyotes
had, most likely, the night before, though
not far enough because the creature lived.

Pete, who carried on his back the welts
of his father's belt, had a near perfect ear
for silence, and so my best friend, this time
threw back his head and made some kind
of unholy screech, voicing the quarrel
the animal could no longer make.

My own throat bubbled with vomit,
as if from that sink hole there
when I plunged, then walked
the dull blade of my pocket knife
up the corded artery of the neck.

We sat there half a lost afternoon,
quiet, not understanding yet,
how we'd chosen to love
what God would not.

SPARROWS

Few believe in angels anymore unless, perhaps,
       in the history of their indifference,
hanging, as they did, between two worlds.
       For a time, as a child, I imagined them with
the small, unsentimental faces street kids have, old
       like that, and a little hungry and long past
thinking of you as doing anything about it,
       or that they slept in sleeves of cardboard
marked Westinghouse. I'd seen them in an alley
       pull a softened wino to his knees and sometimes
caught what seemed a last flaring of their faces passing
       in the evening windows of a cross-town bus.
Walking home from school, late, I'd move beneath the black
       forked trees of winter and not look up, knowing
they slumped there in the branches, and hearing
       the cheep of birds I thought somehow theirs.
I put one in an essay once and Sister Agatha Ann
       closed my right eye, blue, with a smart
hooking slap I'd not thought she had in her and so that
       I had to confess my fervent hope for her
sudden death; drowning I thought seemly and appropriate,
       her dark gown flowering as she sank
in a kind of backwards baptism, maybe somewhere in a canal.
       There in that cold room after the last bus
had huffed my comrades down Divisadero, the radiator
       popping as it cooled, I chalked
I believe in the communion of saints…
       until I thought I'd always stood there at that board,
alone, and so went back to pictures, spare trees
       I roughed out quickly, faces hung like lanterns,
and sparrows, flocks of them snowing down
       like leaves, unnamed, uncounted.

BROTHER

It's the moon and the stars I'm asking,
stalking them through pine and maple,
for a sign or the gentlest of intimations.
But my tongue is the wing
of another dead sparrow
with no whisper. I can't pray exactly,
only sense passing through me
a starlight that's been falling this way for centuries
like salt, some kind of brilliant, crystalline evil,
or worse, it's nothing
but a sensation. Here's the story,
half about my brother,
recently gone to ground,
not getting the right salts
or the full spectrum of light
he needs from Big Pharma
or Big Random or, if you like, Whomever,
who must have taken a wrong turn, again.
Late, I phone and ask after what I already know,
though he still throws me when he answers
that this time the blow was as sudden as an ax
to the head, a stump burning, blowing sparks
and collapsing so it's been like being on fire
but not being able to run out of himself
or keep the long wick of his back
from curling so he's been sitting or walking
around hunched, sometimes pretending to be
working, sometimes just watching others slip
like otters through air slick as water. The hospital
gave him foam slippers and a little white note
for his employer so his sticking around
home now is more than small
pocket heroics, you know, to rise
every day from a bed of ash and hang
near the ceiling that way, for as long
as it's going to take, patient
curling, quiet as smoke.

When he stops speaking, we both read,
imperfectly, the text of our silence.
We both know the weather, the scores,
the stations to go which are many.
We're just trying, hearts trying
by staying here, letting the air go on beating us
about the ears, our pulses beating, fleetingly
in sync, those seconds flaring like comets,
rich with the nearness that saves us.

I CONTINUE

wanting you to know
that some days it's as if my heart inflates the way
I watched an armada of little jelly fish pop
open sails of membrane from their tops and they,
setting out, crossing Monterey Bay. Sometimes,
I am sudden as a jump, parachuting upwards.
Other times, I'm the sharp light I know
in the eyes of the crow that moves overhead
most days, tense and clenching
and unclenching black-fingered wings
before it lights and walks alone by the hidden pond
I knew as a child. Or what about when I stretch out
my arms and just let the leaves and branches accept
the many starlings coming in any old way they want,
which they always do despite my scary metal strips
glancing flashes as if I'm photographing all they eat
and take away each day. It all adds up, not subtracts,
I tell myself, though I go on slamming shut the drawer
of the register in my gut, once for each expenditure.
Yet, there is a flooded field where my heart should be
and you, the allotted water soaking in.
You've come this far, love, come a little farther
past the cage of bones around my chest
that keeps bad things out. Sink low
where the deep water is. You can swim and bob there,
slick as a seal, and I promise that even if one day my head
should be a freeway nexus with its wreckage flared
and smoking, I'll let you out when you want to go.
I'll paint you into the ceiling of the chapel
that arches at the back of my neck when I sit,
eyes closed, stilled, soft candles there, guttering.

NEEDLEPOINT

While dusk's last hour ladders down
the redwood's sticky branches, wrens
that seek a home for one night's wintering
gather like constellations of thought to sweep in
abruptly, lighting in the limbs, chattering until
they fold the small envelopes of their wings and calm.
It's easy, watching March give way to April,
imagining this tree, planted years ago,
as shelter for my mind that's bearing in tonight
from many miles, over the coastal range,
down long fields combed black by plows,
to course near, skittish and
unsure, along the rooftops' edges.

Evenings, things cross over, the bats' looping, palsied scrawls
across the darkened blue, scarves of wood smoke the chimneys'
loose, though no clouds tonight, nor the souls some imagine.
There's a hollow in the trunk, the size a small fist would make
punched into a pillow, the place I made as a child
inside myself for things I grieved, everything I was told
to let go for good like this wind's long drifting.
The tree points out the stars looking finely nettled
and thorny so, if you could, you'd handle them carefully
because they're sharp and can't last, because it's
only loveliness that hurts to lose.

April my mother died, propped
like a doll by the special pillows of needlepoint
I'd watched her make in a rented hospital bed.
The lumps she allowed I touch and that gave her eyes
their lacquered look felt to me just a few runt onions going bad.
The day she left for good I was late, wandering from school,
distracted by the leaves, tiny fists unfurling, curious
about the snails' small armadas crossing the rain-slick walks.

That spring's quiet surprise
was that my father never spoke of her.
Maybe he thought the times he held my eyes with his,

dead light there traveling out into mine
was the full measure of my need, or maybe he couldn't
think about anybody anymore. That year I helped him
and my uncles, clearing orchards of figs planted
long ago in the yellow hills of grass that swell
toward the coastal range on the far side of the valley.

Pleasure for a boy was laying in a saw just above the trees'
arthritic knuckles. Sometimes the wood, knotted and thick,
would baulk, buck me to my knees, and the chained teeth
rip free until they bit the ground, shuddered still, to leave me
shaking, tired, yet somehow proud, too, that I could handle
a world I knew now could be killing. And I'd not complained.

Most birds fled at the machine's first ratcheting. Though
sometimes the chicks of sparrows, jays, wood peckers,
spotted as the chests of Indian ponies,
white and orange and black, were shook to squeaking in their nests,
and floundering, drew down the adults to try to blind us with a beak
or snip an ear, the flickers feigning hurt, stuttering in the air
to draw us off.

But work is work, and we could build
an acre of twisted waste in a day, piece the bigger
limbs for stove wood, truck it off and burn the rest.
The birds stayed and shrieked, wreathing above
the rolling smoke while I watched, a man-boy lost, and harder
ever after to find, some of my parts gone
out into the eyes of birds,

the flame-licked limbs, the smoke.
I gathered them into the chamber that I needed and so had constructed,
neatly, behind my heart. But they don't stay put and like all I've lost,
fly in and out, quickly as my mother's hand-looped stitches.
On a night like this, I see about this tree, shadows
the size of hands coming and going, and feel, as each reaches
the apex of its swing, the thread pulled tight
and then, again, the needle homing.

THE ANOREXIC

I do not like to love
a thing that goes.
Everything goes.
For a long while
I wouldn't visit the niece
with hips she'd made slim enough
to force a father's glance
to fall away.

Forced now into a room
with family, she skitters, mute,
eyes, sunk into her face like votive
candles nearly spent, glassy,
lit with panic.

The first time I saw
her smallest version
of herself, I could only nod
and press a twenty-dollar bill
into her hand,
though I admired her resolve,
firmer than mine,
to say nothing, to leave.
It seemed something

pressed from the eyes
in too rich a distillation, and my eyes
teared involuntarily because
I didn't embrace her,
didn't want to be the child
who pets a wild thing to death.

At night, troubled hungry,
I move down the hall
past the lasso of lamplight
dropped over her shoulder,
a moth thrumming madly
against the shade.

She sketches at her desk.
She looks up as if listening.
She has not seen me.
Her heart may fail her.
My heart may fail her.

I look away.
I won't keep watch
while she goes on
with pinched face,
erasing, erasing.

ANOTHER EVENING INTERLUDE

I am sitting in the yard watching an early evening

blanket my lap and my ankles, watching
sparrows flit by, though thinking of the portly

Edwardian pigeons I know the city is poisoning
where they roost atop the grain silos above Divisadero.

Below them is the wide canal that twists through town.
Below, the ex-cons rubbing cars and trucks at the car wash
toss the dead ones into a can.

At dusk the red light pours easily over the fences,
roof rats scoot in fits and starts, beads
crossing the telephone lines, racking time.

My black-hooded terrier whines and trembles,

and I am sitting here swallowing back a few small barks
and what feels like the hollow bones of wrens,
a wasp nest of paper.

I hear doves.
I think I could coo.
I think I could've been poisoned.

I think I have lived here too long,
listing my sorrows
for anyone to see

and fault me should they care.

How often have I broken
bread with the quick, small birds
dropping near. There, that one is *Joy*,
there, his twin, *Terror*.

I close my eyes and recall the old fools
who drank a little too much wine
standing near the temple gates,
mendicant, holy,
and think, I may have got it wrong.
Maybe it's time I bury a plaster Francis
of Assisi—the way the realtor said,
or was it St. Joseph? —sell the property,

move to the desert and give myself up

to all that burning overhead,
electric, that city, asylum of fat
chance with its shrieking
and the everywhere dying
odor of cigarette smoke, disinfectant, urine.

I could live on discounted dinner rolls, pads of butter,
fried eggs and onions.

I could think of myself as an unemployed Hollywood
extra, keep it a secret,

wear sunglasses,
ride the smooth elevators,
letting my mind,

as if out of ancient, dead seas,
glide the hotel corridors, contained,

like a dark manta ray.

~

TWIN

Always a moment behind and weak, I never sought your visions,
        loving the calm I found
in a blank page, and having always to use these strokes of black
        to offset it, I lose it. This evening they could be
fence posts tacked out in snow, the wobbled paw prints
        of a poisoned fox, the drift that builds
against the ridge come this time of year when you
        drained the warm gutters
of your wrists, unstopped the tub's one hole and vanished.
        Tonight, I am like the man who goes down, confounded,
onto his knees at a revival, blubbering because it's come to this
        and partly because he knows
in the moment of collapse, it'll never take. Why a nail? Unless
        what you needed was something
that could pierce you once and wholly, exactly at the fleshed
        inch of silence. It's why the man
comes forward. Why now and here, next to a highway, a gravel
        parking lot, the car left idling,
the door sagged open in surrender of his one or two beliefs
        before First Pentecost.
Behind that place, its broken voices cracking into song, blackbirds
        fleeing before him, he crosses
a field to sink knee-deep like wreckage in the muddied slush
        and splayed arms of storm-downed trees.
I want to tell you I am sorry and afraid I've grown smaller
        than the measure of my life, that I wake
and dress each day only as I am in the habit of it, my heart, your
        heart, that you once said was a clock
with the works so worn you'd hear them scrape as the hours locked.
        The doors in the house of God
blow loose and the faithful stumble out, the dull bells of their voices,
        wind-snatched, calling, *Brother,*
where'd you go? Cold shadows grow out of his hands in the shapes
        of foxes, and lying there,
it's only snow that fills his mouth now, perfectly

CAFÉ DISSERTATION

Should I have asked? I did love
when you reached across the wide,
circular table of the booth you let me have,
my books, my bits of paper,
curling off the edges like some
accountant who couldn't afford office rent.
That long stretch to place my cup
was so I could see there was still beauty
in those breasts, that real blonde hair
so neatly tucked, saved for some right fellow,
some father for the two kids you had

sleeping in that rusted orange Ranchero
in the parking lot one day you came in just
to get your check and your engine's hiccup
soothed. You showed them to me, as if
to say, *Do you know what you'd be asking if you ask?*
your face pinched like a child's, opening up
when it was just the carburetor stuck and you
the means to take them wherever it was you went.
They never even moved, that girl, that little man,
sleeping, bound, like pupae, in white blankets,
trusting dreams would set them free.
You kept my table for nothing
that long, poor winter of wild scribbling.

It was as if you understood that what I did
needed doing first. I remember rain
fell a lot; it was a fallen world. I even asked
around the way those who grow up with cattle will,
toeing the dirt, staring at the ground
as if a random boot scuff in the dust
might trace a rib or some other sign and found
you came from good stock, married wrong,
but held your own ground, fairly.

Mornings you came to bring my cup,
your eyes, open sky, one knee on the upholstered

seat, your arm grazing mine, electric, as you poured,
as into me, a taste of what could be.
And I, profoundly dumb, useless
with my papers, held up, in each hand,
that afternoon I figured out we would
stay, both of us, attendant to our stations.

Silenced, I watched the wind swinging, dead
cold out of the east, swaying metal signs along
the street, darkening the plate glass windows
so that I could see my face, lean, and staring back
knowing all that was written in that place was writ by rain.

METAL CHRYSANTHEMUMS

He stands at the root of a four-story oak, sunk
     in the lip of a ravine that's
          cut into the back of the rise on the property he's renting,
where rain still beads, strung in long ruts,
          the rusted husk of a Ford pickup
nuzzling some sour-grass and thistle.
         In his helmet, eye plates that are mirrors bristling,
he's some kind of surreal
stage horse, stamping, steam coming off him, brutal
and careless with himself in the unbridled cold.

The white acetylene torches and collides
     with scrap metal and a blue thorn appears
         to probe tiny welds that are clean, born
of a practice that now needs no thought. As he bows
         to his work, his body seems to lean
in a long willing ache, an arc
         of intention and faith. He's told me
he's really white trash at the bone, no kidding, and shit
on the universities, I don't get why you care so much—
the blessings of those bishops?

All the while, his kid running wild
     in an ever-expanding orbit around us cawing
         some oblique and necessary
rooster or peacock noise, face
         a dumb potato
topping a sweatshirt, patches of red dirt—*The schools*
        I could afford couldn't do any more
than make him cry.
A boy isn't metal. I don't try and fix him—
And just as these lines are a quick walk

toward a final noun, he pivots
     round the stalk of his invention
         for the last time, slaps up
his mask and spits, pointing to the tips
         of a weak January sun, burning

on the folds of his metal chrysanthemum,
                  the boy pulled loose of a circumnavigation
beyond reason or beauty, raucous bird, suddenly quiet,
lighting at his father's shoulder, small eyes, sullen,
green as saved pennies.

THESE PARTICULARS OF RAIN

begin with a few, fat spatters
on the windshield of my truck,
then a car wash deluge bringing me
to a crawl until I come to a stop
in the already coursing gutters
somewhere downtown, I'm not sure, exactly,
straining forward in my seat, unable to see,
knuckles of rain thrumming the cab overhead.
I startle at the dark, homeless face
melting on the passenger side's window.
The man knocks and keeps knocking until
even the dried, accordion wings of my heart
start working, and I let go and unlock
what's his side now as he climbs in,
bouncing the seat, grunting,
Comin' all the way down this time, brother,
head nodding to assure me,
his breath, untroubled by teeth,
bringing outdated news of Mogen David
and maybe somebody's discarded egg
salad sandwich. He shivers and shakes the black
strings of his hair, flecking my interior with the foul
nameless bits of his travels, sits staring ahead,
fermenting, a root cellar silence. Finally, he turns,
face a block of white cheese badly hacked,
one eye filmy as an old nickel greased by many fingers.
The other, bright with schizophrenia, I think,
comes into view when he cocks his neck
to study me with a bird's one-eyed intensity
until I'm ashamed that my regret must be obvious.
Then quietly intimate, to me, to himself
he reveals, *Brother, for a minute there,*
I thought we were lost.

WHEELING ABOVE THE DARKENING

parking lots of Nordstrom's and Macy's,
it's the seagulls catching the last light
that give me the beauty
of their white bellies; with these, I'd be
for I am here for beauty, perfume or maybe
a lily or a suit fine enough I could imagine
wearing it, in a pinch, even for my funeral.
There's the beggar, suited in shoes of burlap, planted
at the base of an aluminum light pole as if believing
he'll flower again, face of torn ham and dried,
black jam and his signs with their reasons reminding
me of those half grams of granular hope, that memory
almost taking off all her sweet clothes
right there in the truck. But I'm still trying to push
the door open soberly while the wind keeps gusting
against me, first pins of rain driving into my turned cheek.
Just now I was listening to a broadcast about how dying
makes you more alive than ever and thinking,
Well, there's enough there for a book but not mine
because I have no doubt I was most alive in that garden
hut with the one enormous redwood on the right, another
to its left, the roses there, running renegade and overgrown
along the fence tops and the rotting windowsills,
the raggedy privets everywhere, and I,
in that first heaven of plenty, only twenty and immortal,
time to burn in my vacant solicitation, sitting there getting high
just watching a fly or, often, a wasp, like a small thorn of light
etching the windowpane, my breath coming light
as one dying, spending all what time was mine waiting
for the bidden word to come nestle in my ear, alive
with its right rustle, its honest, memorable sting.

FOR MY FATHER IN HIS AGE

It should be easy sitting in an orchard going dark,
        counting the birds come in.
The almond branches lift, scratching sky
thinned honey-blue as new engine oil.
Yet, each year you feel yourself grown smaller;
        the breath that bells
your lungs weakening.

Summer began early
        its clicking in the dry grass;
blackbirds dropped, quarter notes on the branches
and telephone poles
belting the yellow pasture. The found surprise
        of blackberries twining
across a hill—the shock of such longing again. You almost want it back,

that season so busy with itself.
        But your head finds, too easily now,
the cushion of your chest. The birds bend,
again, again,
like little oil rigs, drilling soil.
        What works these tiny excavations in the mind,
lets loose this dreaming? What lets go?

FIRST RAIN

Soft on the roof and I wakened remembering,
wholly, the storm years back strong enough to blow
heads off small trees, send a few road signs spinning
like scimitars, then the air falling suddenly slack
then winding up again and the rain
twisting in silken ropes from the eaves I stood under
staring past them into sky, trying to find one line,
to follow its travel all the way down
until my mind was falling too,
as if tossed from a plane, no parachute, a man diminishing,

stunned with the gravity of things.
It had begun with gentle though certain
flecks on my face. The first I welcomed,
though withdrew my dawn cup
when the drops went from tentative to a fat plunking
into my coffee. Midmorning I started backing away
from the glass, watching what I could on TV,
sure, then, something was up. Come afternoon
I was considering the chances the weather would break
the back of the bad years in the Sierra

which had killed countless trees doomed by drought beetles
whittling their multitudinous, deep-chambered tombs.
It wasn't exactly biblical, though the wind, insatiate,
had its stories, which have gone their own way for ages,
those endings that give way to beginning again.
When a small levee near Stockton gave way
like the slump of old shoulders, water seeking the low
places, one roadway was river, and the woman
with her two babies in car seats said she wouldn't swim out
without them, 911 recording the last of their high singing.

There's a wild dignity in me that wants to sing, spurred
by the violence of things trying to become themselves
enormously, metamorphous at a cost. The newscaster on air,
helicoptering overhead, actually suggested prayer,
and, you know, no matter what I think of him
Christ's lesson in fidelity was no easy feat.
My own heart still weakens and skips its two-step
too quickly when I don't know what it is trying
to come through, though I go on understanding it
as a kind of chanting that drops well this side of mortality,
which I feel like a boxer going down hard,

braving closely examined failure,
the daily loneliness of rising again.
It was Channel 24 or my mind sending me pictures
of the delta caving in the doors of boat houses and sheds,
walls leaning until they slid and lay all the way over
slowly, the roofs like doffed hats sailing away on the water,
so that my thoughts, disordered for a moment,
caught sight of the holy seal of one home's lone upstairs,
Emily Dickinson window, and my neck twitched when

the dark starling I saw catapulted into that glass.
The last night it slowed, and I rose
to see the night sky drawn
and quartered as it gave way so that
from its center stars stepped out carefully to quiver.
Glancing down I saw worms struggling out
of the old, ill-fitting clothes of soil,
from under the eaves came a dove's, *O, O,*
melting open a hole in the air,
and I entered.

LANDSCAPE WITH DOUBT

Say, for instance, I am looking
at the shed's metal door standing open

at the end of an orchard of stone fruit
prickly with bees. Clouds wrinkle east.

Sun spots the apricots and the plums
dangling like small planets out front

of your window set over the sink.
Could I say then what it is that touches,

like a doctor's hands, these many spots
I'd thought forgotten?

An oil drum brimming heavy with rain,
a shovel head rusted, sunk in the mud—

anchors you don't need anymore.
You were there in the bed and then not.

And all I could think was,
It's a poor design—

no way to open a hospital window.
I would've liked to do so. I suppose

I'm walking for you, now. You're not
even this moth asleep on a leaf that I close

into my hand, its murmur, a dry mouth
on my palm. If I could wrap this minute

in nothing but itself would that be eternity?
If I faced the sky and let my hands fall

open would I feel myself fluttering off?
Could I find you then?

THE BIRD TREE

Come the blue dusk they
are a chattering city above you

in the branches of a spruce,
their shrill cries like thin strips of tin,

chaffing, metal on metal,
wordless and ancient.

Your arms, which were once
fins, twitch at the sight of them.

But you are a man;
to rise would mean hanging from a tree

for a while. And the dying part.
This is happening. Every day

your hands are sore,
and seem to glow with an x-ray's

fluorescence, flinching now
even at the turning of doorknobs.

You watch the god-step in their hop
limb to limb, and name

after name you could give them
and not understand

that purple and green iridescence
glossed over their black, enviable bodies,

the brilliant yellow of their eyes,
black, too, at the centers, and shining.

Moon like a zeppelin, bright
between the leaves, drifts east

toward a bank of storm clouds.
Excited, the birds weave thin ropes of air

around the mast of the tree,
spindled and back-lit

by herds of standing stars.
You approach and the rushing

black surf lifts away. The rain,
heavy as blood, comes down

into the small
spoons of your hands.

STRINGING WIRE

If I could believe that when the morphine quit,
he rose on wings we didn't know he had,
I wouldn't be sitting here
trying to find a name for breath or these sparrows
dropping one by one, as if shot, from my wire.
I might say something for an open sky
running slick as gasoline.
I'm not a young man. I cry
for a couple of minutes and stop
without trying. I think of the Psalms,
the Old Testament and think,
Isaac, temple, furnace.
But I say, *Raven*, loving
the warp of that exhalation,
and the sight of one working now
toward the sycamores along the river.
One night, years back, we drove skirting
the ridge above Oakhurst, lights of that village
gleaming through mist, and he recited
Kipling learned in high school,
said, *Why don't you write
something people could understand?*
Looked over at me smoldering in my seat,
socked me softly. *What's wrong with that?*
I didn't say anything, though now
I'd say, *Wings with the light slipping off,*
or, *Feather*, or, *Somewhere a rustle.*
Maybe, *Quill plucked clean and bleeding.*
Or, *Cattle-lick, swamp cooler, cutters.*
Maybe just, *Shovel. Hammer. Father.*

CATTLE

Even in the blind, blonde days of youth
when I knew nothing of resignation,
cattle gave me pause.
Into the poppies, fiddleheads and plush grasses,
they still pull me wondering what, if anything, flowers
in their brains. Without fences they will wander
as if they feel the ghost buffalos' migration.
The air flares warm around them.
They're just standing, so calm that when the wind
continues asking the grasses to bow, I feel
something like grace. Mostly that's in spring
when my car spins me down the ridge with a fine
spume of rain come early as I take the long way home,
thinking of things that should've worked out, things that might,
beads of longing sliding quietly sideways before the wind
plucks them from the edges of the windshield.
Sometimes on 41, speeding into evening,
I'll see them, heads and forelegs picking up
as they hurry home in a gallows line over foothill paths,
hoof-stamped with inkwells of dark,
stopping some to water, then moving on past the hides of coyotes,
flagging their warning from the fanged wire fences.
Come winter, sitting in my vestibule of silence, high
on the edge of the road, I'll shut my engine off and crack
the windows just to feel the air ribbon sharply
in and out of my lungs. I'll watch them, circled in groups,
make a fence of their flanks to block
the wind that needles them, hear them moo
in the low wholesomeness of the psalms,
or sad cellos, music I must have known once
because it's left a little hole in my side that then brims.
Brighter days, they move from place
to place, translating their given pastures into themselves,
the sure machinery of their jaws
sliding side to side, eyes half-lidded,
minds blank as Bodhisattvas
though not the same as they've nothing to divest.
Is it my steady and ordered life,

its certain itinerary, its many clocks,
that affords me this jumping off place?
Years ago, I watched some herded into a chute, restless
with what I was sure was an intimation of the end.
One tried to climb the rails that guided them, clattered
and thrashed, bellowing in a way that was mostly surprise
as it sensed that betrayal that will fall through
all of us one day, like this Judas sun now plunging
through the stricken trees with a final,
inevitable *No*, though it won't be anything
we haven't known in lessor fashion,
at the smaller stations of our passing.

NOCTURNE

After the cattle plod home in darkness,
and the stars wheel into place,

I pick my way down to study the river.
It's low, just a murmur pouring

through roots of willows, rocks of granite.
Wind sends some pine needles sideways,

and my eyes drift up and see light from the city
is a bridge spanning blackness.

I realize I've abandoned all plans to make a home here.
There's no time for that. Regret, and a plan.

Riffles run the surface of the water like an unnamed desire
that fans up the neck, and I climb the ridge

to the truck and drive away slowly, thinking how
I've been looking, always reading, then, recently,

the doctors' dark conclusions making my mind suddenly
clear as water, like today when I came out of the trees

to find deer, feeding quietly along a stream.

IT GOES ON

My sister has the new valve
puckering and unpuckering
and feels it, a soft goldfish syllable
that bubbles and pops in her breast.
That's just imagination, she says.
The doctors swear you couldn't feel it
unless something was seriously wrong.

I'm thinking of the pig, unharvested, floating
above Battersea Power Station on the cover
of the Pink Floyd album that came out
when we were still young as we cross
the parking lot of City Mercy, post-op,
and I'm still looking up, the high ashes
or sparrows or maybe my mind making faint
letters of sentences that once held answers,
unwinding over the high, flat industrial roofs,
then spreading until they aren't there anymore.

Home, she wants me to look
for the source of the high-pitched whine
that began some months ago
like the sky's own tinnitus coming from the east,
probably her neighbor's wireless computers
or electric fence or some of his ham radio
shit, though now she can't tell;
the best she can figure is that it exists
about thirty feet overhead in the northeast corner of her lot.

All I can do is spin slowly and confirm it.

She needs medication. She needs it all;
I can't ask. She needs to lie down;
she needs to stop talking
about that whine entering her bones
at the harsh angle of hospital needles.
She says, It's the persistence that gets you.

In college my roommate had a budgie that no one
knew could talk until one night—after we'd been up
eighty-something hours editing a 16mm thesis
that cost his new Ford Mustang and all I might have
eaten that winter and spring—when that bird
started up, *You're gonna cry ninety six tears,*

You're gonna—and kept at it
until we jammed it into a shoebox
and slid it outdoors to make it or not, which it didn't,
grey and stiff in its tux and yellow cummerbund,
hard enough to throw overhand for good
into the ice-locked alley come morning.

Going in I say, Maybe. Though, I'm not aware
of spirits that can live in the holes of the shadowed eaves,
just the little ovens of swallows,
just the thrum of thin wings.
In a bedroom she's painted blue, I see her lips are blue.
I put my arms under her knees. I arrange her.
I cross her hands over her chest, place her face to the east.
I do everything lightly, the way when their hair is washed,
I imagine the heads of the dead are lifted gently.

You have to find that sound, she says, beginning to slip.
I stand there awhile, until awhile is too long:
the distance her breath has to travel.
How could we have boxed that bird for singing
what might have felt its first sudden truth?
Later, outside, I spin slowly, slack-jawed,
sounding with the bones of my head but
can't source it. There's no direction,
just a wire-whine, a raw singing
that comes out of nowhere and goes on.

ALREADY NOVEMBER

That day after the appointment
the crows in the empty parking lot looked
like nineteenth century doctors, frocked
in black and arrogant. Yet, they were more
just as they were, birds at the top of a pole
dropping sounds of rasps working metal.
Though I never think of them abandoning
themselves to the wind the way a gull will
kite easily or starlings spiral into columns
of smoke, something in me wishes it knew
how to caw back to them and all
that fall out of the sky. I felt like a boy
looking up from a book, mouth open, a cup,
brimmed. Here, now, if I were to pray
it would be to a crane or an owl or, maybe,
one of these portly Edwardian pigeons
dressed in vests of green and subtle purple,
strutting the gutters of Divisadero
below the one set of grain silos
left standing in the middle of town.
They roost in what was the caretaker's shack
built at the top, its glinting windows small
as teeth from this distance, mostly broken,
the sheet metal walls finely pitted with rust.
I've come home to sit for a while in that shade,
tracks of the Southern Pacific at my back,
before me the canal rushing away,
the one gull blown inland by a storm
scavenging over it low, then rising.
A priest told me prayer was mostly listening,
and faith, nothing more or less than persisting
until the spirit arrives. Oh, I said, *That*:
the white sheet, then the keyboard's wild clicking.
Hey bird, lofting above the soft applause of your wings,
bird who may know the way to Argentina or
God-knows-where, I can't help feeling
once we crossed over a sea, shallow
and briny, broad as a desert, hot wind

slicking our smooth feathered heads.
I can't help knowing neither of us was
constructed to survive. Already it's November
and the crooked architecture of trees laid bare.
I think, if you winter over this year,
you will come to my window. If you go,
once more, one I loved will have passed.
I will think of your wings taking the blues of
morning. And that praying which is waiting?
It's me imagining the pain radiating
from my shoulder blades is only the first
of the old feathers, uncertain in their unfolding.

~

KEEPING TIME

Outside, in the hung clothes, the wind kicks
up the legs of my Levis, my long Johns twisting
madly like a fellow that was just asking
for straitjacketing, unable, I guess, to strangle
back one sorrow or another.
And inside, there's that little hut in my head
made for cover over the wells dug last summer
until the rig punched through
to the underground river that pumps itself up
so cold it'll crimp the blood vessels of my forehead
until I cry out, even in sleep. Not the living
water within nor this troubled dancing
outside is exactly the whole of things
though I spend my time trying to fit them.

This winter I've taken to sleeping on old wrestling mats
dragged out to keep my spine,
made over into cigar ash, from crumbling
and to accommodate angels or memories of one
whom I wanted to help most but couldn't.
It was her hair falling thin as corn silk
or January light that showed me how easy it was
dropping into a cold that stays with you. I can't stop God
turning another cliché. But I won't be turning
up the gas, I won't be optioning that story. It's no good living
with a thing like that readied in your heart's pocket.
Having done it all my life, I can wait. I'll wear
a knit cap, keeping what heat I have left
from leaving too soon off the top of my head.

I'll tuck my dachshund around my feet like a warm wine sack
and let the weather build.
The animal's ankles twitch, mine twitch; we make good time.
Like this, ten years will pass same as any afternoon
watching dark anvils of rain stacked on the horizon, forcing
me in, come sundown, glad to put myself away, carefully,
like a right tool, well used.

I've done my time, those ten thousand hours of devotion
same as trying to whistle precisely, wanting
to mimic that whine the wind makes where it catches
the torn corners of the shed's metal roof.
This I keep doing for reasons firm as the pleasure of watching
my far neighbor's eucalyptus darken as it gathers the last ravens
from the sky and, then, the kerchiefs of clouds drawn
over the face of an early moon leaving shadows
that pass over, here and then not. It's that here and then not
business that's the author. But you already know
there's a business end, even to this, our gentle endeavor.

And I like this which I'm allowed, which I read Theresa of Avila
called the "consolation of gusts," that is for me just the wind
playing again, this time a flock of kazoos, or is it the throats
of mud ducks, paddling overhead, out
to meet evening again. Rain
has stopped plinking into the buckets of my lungs,
and I don't seem to be coughing, and my wifi's up and running
again so I may be righting myself soon
sure, now, there's a signal
I hear singing.

Not long and I'll be getting up as if just reincarnated
as a fox or a possum stealing outside on little black feet,
a little excited, following the voices of the river down
where animals gather at dusk.
I'll plunge in and come clambering out on the far side,
a low-bellied horse, sliding my teeth side to side, snorting
and stamping in the wet weeds and dark, knowing
only of fetlocks dripping, flanks shuddering,
something that needed doing, done.

THE SPECIFICS OF AIR

Tufts of arrows, bark-brown,
are the sparrows I call
with store-bought seed,
every evening, making my
amends. I love to see them
loading the little socks of their bodies.
I wish they could show me
how I might lay down
all that I carry, to live
on next to nothing, to make
those subtle translations of air.
As a boy, I'd shoot them, the killing
methodic, casual, very pleasant.
I'd pour a small pillowcase
full with their warmth,
that heft the new dead have,
fling it into a canal,
sun squeezed off the horizon
like an eye swelling shut, first red,
then yellowed-blue, finally black.
At times, the earth turns
too quickly. Since my diagnosis,
I've been practicing my absence
the way my neighbor draws
a bow across the wide hips
of his cello, never maudlin,
though piercing, the pauses
ever longer as he decides
which notes to keep,
which are unneeded.
I would like, when it comes,
a silence as interesting as that.
At twenty, alcoholic, wobbly,
in love, I followed you,
dark-lashed nurse of my longing,
down the wards, watching you
pet the old ones dying there,
racked like moths, pinned,

though still humming, great-eyed,
and soft with their sweet talcum smells.
How they would drive us, sometimes,
out to the river bank come lunch
to rasp our bodies raw, needing, then
to believe in the future.
One day we fell apart
to lie on our backs, open-handed, spent,
and it seemed the old souls came down
with the birds, all around us.
I'd like to think you'd remember,
someday should you need,
grace, falling like that,
quiet as leaves.

COME NIGHTFALL

I'm at the house
in the pillaged neighborhood
my mother-in-law won't leave. I enter, quiet
as one of the crack house mystics I passed on the corner,
waiting for his measure of heaven, shifting his feet, rolling

his shoulders like a boxer staying warm, blowing what was left
of himself into his hands for company, maybe, a sign

of a body still near. I move down the hallway's tunnel of dark
                                        towards the light of the television,
flickering. Small in her deep, pillowed chair,
swathed in electric blue afghans, she's a princess demanding,

Who the fuck are you? Her language has gone
course, sand she spits times she's aware she hasn't any taste for this
not knowing what's going on anymore. And Tommy, ancient
          rat terrier, squirms into existence from one sleeve
of her robe, draws back his lips to show the remains
        of his teeth. He quivers,

and rattles his throat as if he thinks whatever is coming for them has
shown. But all her life she was a swimmer and strong: she's stuck
here so long now the good sense sifts out of her,

bit by bit, so that I think of the termites in her walls incessantly
excreting onto the baseboards tiny, exquisite piles the vacuum sucks
come Thursday next or, if not then, the week after, if the man comes,

the half-ruined vet hired to clean—though she thinks his mumbling
some kind of Kaddish and threatens to call the cops every time.
I want to know if she wouldn't like a bath
or her Golden Girls DVD found? She wants to know

Who are you to ask? though she accepts the Spaghetti O's
she insists on like a kid, purse of her mouth pulling
tight over the spoon I hold, her eyes on mine and, then
downcast as the girl of fifteen she suddenly is.

Then it's a half-hour of the Bible read out plainly, tonight—
Old Testament quarrels with God. After, she takes the book from my hand
and explains though Tommy can't grasp it, he's going, *Up there,*
since any fool can see an animal has feelings, same as us. I think
the logic is sound though inverted.

I can see all that her self was, isn't any longer.

I don't like her like this, making me think,
involuntarily, as I do now, of my sweet German shepherd,
gut full of tumors like turnips left to rot in a sack.

Last week we laid him down. We said, *It's all right, buddy,* his eyes,
sagged and knowing, trusting as any eight-year-old. We said, *Good,*
pressing the sharp needle in, the vet saying quickly
that the animal wasn't with us anymore. I knew he wasn't there

or anywhere any longer so tonight I already know she's right:
the dog and I are the same. And both needing a good piss
we take to the yard. I don't have any trouble understanding the stars
as dying light shook out like the sounds of tambourines fading,
so far from us, they say, it's hard to tell the living from the dead.

                    It's beneath those thistles of brilliance the dog and I finish
up damaging some azaleas before we look and see
an armful of late geese vectoring suddenly over her lot,
one hard bought, plot of harsh ghetto light.

It's their long, certain pull I can't explain, it's their calls'
curt passing I question, it's the swiftness of the cold, invisible
river that floats their hushed wings. They go and I go

on listening out into untraveled space
when from out of the dark house, in shrill whisper
comes Job's only answer tonight,

Who are you to ask?

Who the fuck are you?

HOLIDAY

My Rose of Sharon has gone dormant,
thin and spindly as
the many masts of sailing ships
gone to port in winter
that I've seen in paintings,
so in the black flowers of my days
I'll be a long time waiting
for summer and its lavender napkins
to be waving their rare promise.
It'll be some time before my company
of wasps is returning to their small pueblos
tucked under the wooden struts of the fence.
Evening, and I'm standing near the smoking
pile of compost with a flashlight watching
for new things and thinking of myself
weighed down by dirt. Cold,
I'll have to go in, probably watch Jimmy Stewart,
stuttering to run a Savings and Loan
and dark Barrymore in his chair, scrunching
his bushy eyebrows, clutching his rumpled blankets,
a familiar story helping us cross over the river
where feelings try to rise like drowned bodies
worn, now, unspecific, pale and lumpy.
At times I can't help wishing a different life
where I mastered a second language
or learned to make a cello moo precisely.
What I am doing is trying to get out of the way,
grow small enough to gust high
as ashes blowing east
come another dawn's decent wind.
What I'm doing is trying to make
these little constructions collapse easily
down to the deepest margin of my page.
I know late, again, I'll be scanning my papers,
arranging the light here and then there, lifting
my sharpest of scissors, putting them down,
taking care with my fingers.
For now, I'll be awhile standing

for nothing but myself,
with my one hand glowing,
breath blossoming into air, just feeling
the good suspicion of my neighbors,
just watching the moon
slip another cloud-braided halter,
just prodding this word or that
where it lies in my head
like a flatulent ass or an ox
that's not minding the flecks of blood
all around but just chewing the night straw
burning like gold from the lips.

IT'S LIKE THIS

Coming when I call, my nieces,
two fortune-tellers, wet heads wrapped
in towels, sit down with their tumble
of questions nearly fitting the puzzle
I've made of myself. Yes, they're ready;
offering their hands, palms up and clean,
they clamor like the high thin echoes after clappers
striking small bells that needed ringing, and no we will not
watch TV while we eat; you aren't Laura Croft, you're human.
Put the knife down; you don't know but outside there's
one of those sunsets going down like a burning freighter
or the slump at the end of a decade and the light sucked up
like the last of your milkshake, and soon enough your body
will be heavy with adolescence, your head resting in your hands
like the pope praying for the conversion of Russia
and Mother Mary doing it because she liked him, and that's
very like a parent to play favorites so don't forget forgiveness.
Let's think about Isaac a little and Abraham, also; let's
thank the Holy Spirit, a very good writer, because you will
have to give up, and then you'll have to keep trying, and
hey, now, you'll need to slow down and do this
with a little dignity; we might want to say grace,
calling it down like light rain after heavy weather or sometime
when you'll want to go to your knees or throw your head
back watching a jet fighter vectoring east over the desert
on a crisp morning, afterburners pulling hard right out of your heart.
There are children who would slit your throat for that pizza
so go on eat, but take your time because you'll have to eat it all.

THE ORGAN DONOR

I'll be back, and appreciated, maybe,
my heart carried down an avenue I loved
like a heavy plum riding high in the breast
pocket of, say, a woman who, almost dead,
came to understand all is extra-
ordinary. It's possible: the afterlife
is imagined in ten thousand ways.
Yes, say she has a child, specific,
say, with Down syndrome.
And the boy needs her hand to quiet him,
as she can today. And aren't they walking,
and isn't she thinking she must often make
a fine misreading of the text in his eyes
because he only brightens at the simplest things
though he seems to understand them completely?
There is the silver and blue aluminum balloon
in the store window and, then, falling briefly
to one knee, he taps the wriggling horns
of snails, persistent as Bedouin, caravanning
along the gutter's wet oasis. Look, here's a full stop
where an unshaven stranger has dropped
entirely into a book, his café table roofing
a Shar Pei in its accordion coat turning
its gaze to appraise the child. Satisfied,
it rests its head on its paws. It blinks, once,
and again, and then is gone back into the little
deaths boredom makes. Across the street, the park
with the cathedral's empty bell tower
lets go a sudden clatter of pigeons overhead,
and the boy throws back his head, eyes swinging
with them, and he, mouthing, *Ohhhhh,*
as if birthing wonder for the first time. And, again,
that little kicking in her chest.

HUMMINGBIRD

I thought it was a large moth, mistook it
for a portent of something special
in the wind:
a dusky desert brother
to the red darts usually seen.
It looked down on its luck,
then up again, down,
then, with a pirouetting loop,
penned the air in a grand sweeping
signature to the left.
Its is a rapier's thrust, a phlebotomist's
needle probing before setting deep.
Its very name could be, Sudden.
Like now,
in front of my window, it makes the sign
of the cross then,
heart the size of a pea,
it delves and it suckles,
thistles of light where
the wings ought to go,
where the heart goes. That quick.
That tentative. That sure.

AND YOU WILL WAKE

Beyond the rotting fence
and the gate that leans,
    banging in the wind

in fits and starts
    like a sleepy drunk about to collapse,

    beyond the wild mustard and the sunflowers
and the bulrush choking a little dogleg of a creek,
    you could find, if you looked,

the huge, black bees that drone there
    like old Messerschmitts in sun-polished air.

    There is something
just below the floating illusion
    of cloud shadows wrinkling the pond's face.

And when I watch a red-tailed hawk
    oar slowly over the lake, brushing

    the top of it, its talons half in the dark water, half
in the bright pennies spread over the surface,
    it rises, passing over me, standing

on that shore, transfigured by its grace,
    as it mounts with little pushups

    its staircase of air, more specific
than any symbol,
    greater than any dream.

EVENING

Walking it seems each day
less far, and now nearing home,

we see the storm-lit sky
and the bare sapling of our yard,

silver and grey in that changing light.
My wife says how soon

warmth will raise the little flags
of leaves and they unfurl.

But, first the rain, the near-killing frosts.
The house is cold and dark.

In the doorway, we hesitate,
looking back. The lowering sky,

the single, naked tree.

ENOUGH

I'm looking for mushrooms that blacken
in secret. And underground rivers
       that course for God-knows-how
many miles seem this evening
to be working in me. The dead
clog these waters, and memory is
an eye that can't see them clearly anymore.
No moon, high clouds. I wish there were geese
flying over or even a satellite's tiny flaring.
As a boy I could believe just by walking
into the trees I might become
any of the animals living
there alone in rough burrows, letting
their lives spool out without perfection.
Night, and dew sparks the tips
of maples patterned like Pleiades,
       genuine stars that stay yoked
to their course as if for a reason.
I know old men can become children
threading shadows—
only their own compassion
walking ahead as if to turn
to meet them someplace farther where
the sun will set these woods on fire.
       Last night I dreamt of crossing over
Wyoming on a road plunging west
and coming on a bluff of smooth,
darkened boulders, lightening licking
out, horizontally, from some
hammer-headed clouds above them.
I thought of you,
       who once saved my life,
who set her heart like a snapped
locket on my falling
into this world the way
a swallow might drop exhausted
by the storm's leaden rain,

and I, young, just driving,
        homing, knowing it
was enough.

THE WIDOWER

Sundays were to take summer
on the tongue, mornings
in bed, black jam and biscuits,
the butter spilled freely and trickling,

sooner or later, tracing
the line of her thigh
to the low places and that whorl
that slips into underground rivers.

When they walked, she'd held his hand
as if he were a boy in need of leading
out of a dim, pine wood
toward home's yellow windows.

Sometimes there is an answer.
Sometimes there is a person
who's a guiding word come down daily,
certain as a mythical spot of blood out of the sky

or a bird thumping the window
in an end stop perfected.

Now, long days he tries not to think
of her. Forgets, finds an early letter,
and she saying, *Come. The sun
is hammering here, but there's some rain,*

*and this breeze that comes
up after midnight.
Many stars.*

He naps. All day
The duct of his heart
fills with hummingbird blood.
All day the weather comes in.

It seems she must have been shopping,
comes tapping the window,

again with her wet pockets of darkness,
again with her little packages
of darkness
tied with string and balanced under an arm,

mouth, soft as pebbles
of rain pelting soil.
He doesn't go to the door.
He knows there isn't a door.

Later, the sky emptied and clear,
he wanders out under a moon
that seems it could cut, sharp as glass,
feels guilty being there

still loving so much just the sound
of a train shuffling in the distance.

WHEN THE CLOCKS

find these hours
at the bottom of my years

and a glacier moon
courting silence reveals

ants pillaging the purse
of a dead wren's chest,

when needles of stars pin me, stilled,
when I'm sure the mosquito is the fallen world

and my heart lurches like a frog out of wet grass
to rest three feet away blinking at me without recognition,

I sit on the wooden porch until morning,
old songs crowding the back of my throat.

THE DISTANCE

Besides the halo of a distant town
      or stars netted in pines,
black, set far up on a ridge,
      there seems little to report
from the windows of a passing train.
      You see the cold moon sails
a sea of grass someone parted with their knees,
      wading out, the line, just glimpsed,
and somehow grave because it fails suddenly,
      and so that you wonder who lies there,
or for how long, no evidence of him
      or her having trailed back.
Didn't you, once, want to cut your own
      line out, even if it was only to shout back,
No, not this way. Didn't you
      want to part the fabric of the world?
Recall unzipping your girl's jeans,
      a warm spring rain, and you descending
into that brief church the tall grass made.
      How did you know you'd never be the same—
not nineteen and leaving home for good.
      Wasn't it the way she kept opening
and closing her eyes to those splinters of rain
      to look at you as for the first time
that scared you, seeing how close love was
      to loss? And hasn't it always been?
And, now, the train hurtling the distance
      and the porter smiling with beautiful teeth
leaning to offer the consolation of a gin
      though memory briefly offers you the same,
before the windows go abruptly dark
      as you fly, entering thickets and the trees.

D. James Smith's work has appeared in *Blackbird, The Malahat Review, Notre Dame Review, Poetry International, Stand* and many other journals. A Booklist Top Ten First Novel Pick, a nominee for the Pen/ Faulkner and a finalist for The Northern California Book Award, he is the recipient of the Edgar Allen Poe Award as well as a fellowship in poetry from the National Endowment for the Arts. He holds MA degrees in Counseling and English and lives in California's central valley where he studied with Philip Levine.

Grateful acknowledgment goes to the editors of these magazines where these poems or earlier versions of them first appeared:

Asheville Poetry Review: "The Bird Tree," "Letter;" *Art Life*: "I Was Only;" *Artful Dodge*: "Metal Chrysanthemums;" *Blue Mesa Review*: "Winter;" *Borderlands, The Texas Poetry Review*: "Specifics of Air," "West Valley Dog;" *Brooklyn Review*: "Enough;" *Canary*: "Cattle," "First Rain;" *Cape Rock*: "Café Dissertation," "Come Nightfall;" *Chicago Quarterly Review*: "When the Clocks;" *Clackamas Review*: "The Distance;" *Cold Mountain Review*: "Nocturne;" *Comstock Review*: "Sparrows;" *Confrontation*: "Landscape with Doubt;" *Connecticut River Review*: "The Organ Donor;" *Cumberland River Review*: "Hummingbird;" *Cutbank*: "The Insomniac;" *Exit 7*: "I Continue;" *Florida Review*: "These Particulars of Rain," "Wheeling above the Darkening;" *Hawaii Pacific Review*: "For My Father in His Age;" *Mudfish*: "Needlepoint;" *Owen Wister Review*: "It Goes On;" *Oxford Magazine*: "Rain In The Fence;" *Painted Bride Quarterly*: "Neighbor;" *Permafrost*: "Stringing Wire;" *Potomac Review*: "Twin;" *Quarterly West*: "Another Evening Interlude," "Brother;" *Quercus Review*: "The Anorexic;" *Poetry Canada Review*: "And You Will Wake;" *Sensitive Skin Magazine*: "The Calf," "Holiday," "It's Like This," "Rain & I;" *Slant*: "Absence;" *Soundings East*: "Already November;" *Talking River Review*: "Evening;" *Willow Review*: "Keeping Time."

Thank you to the National Endowment for the Arts for a grant which helped make this book possible.

Thank you, also, to Charles and Gail Entrekin whose keen attention made the book better, and then, who kindly made it happen.

And to Max Blagg who always points the way.

HIP POCKET PRESS MISSION STATEMENT

It is our belief that the arts are the embodiment of the soul of a culture, that the promotion of writers and artists is essential if our current culture, with its emphasis on media and provocative outcomes, is to have a chance to develop that inner voice and ear that express and listen to beauty. Toward that end, Hip Pocket Press will continue to search out and discover poets and writers whose voices can give us a clearer understanding of ourselves and of the culture which defines us.

OTHER BOOKS FROM HIP POCKET PRESS

You Notice the Body: Gail Rudd Entrekin (poetry)

Terrain: Dan Bellm, Molly Fisk, Forrest Hamer (poetry)

A Common Ancestor: Marilee Richards (poetry)

Sierra Songs & Descants: Poetry & Prose of the Sierra:
   Gail Rudd Entrekin, Editor

Truth Be Told: Tom Farber (epigrams)

Songs for a Teenage Nomad: Kim Culbertson (young adult fiction)

Yuba Flows: Kirsten Casey, Gary Cooke, Cheryl Dumesnil, Judy Halebsky, Iven Lourie, & Scott Young; Gail Rudd Entrekin, Editor (poetry)

The More Difficult Beauty: Molly Fisk (poetry)

Ex Vivo (Out of the Living Body): Kirsten Casey (poetry)

Even That Indigo: John Smith (poetry)

The Berkeley Poets Cooperative: A History of the Times:
   Charles Entrekin, Editor (essays)

Jester: Grace Marie Grafton (poetry)

The Occasionist: Curt Anderson (poetry)

Storyland: Keith Dunlap (poetry)

WEB PUBLICATIONS

Canary, a Literary Journal of the Environmental Crisis:
hippocketpress.org/canary

Sisyphus, Essays on Language, Culture & the Arts:
hippocketpress.org/Sisyphus

www.ingramcontent.com/pod-product-compliance
Lightning Source LLC
LaVergne TN
LVHW091231080426
835509LV00009B/1239